DATE DUE		

When the
Earth
Moves

Earthquakes
and Volcanoes

First published in Australia in 2008 byYoung Reed
an imprint of New Holland Publishers (Australia) Pty Ltd
Sydney • Auckland • London • Cape Town

1/66 Gibbes St Chatswood NSW 2067 Australia
218 Lake Road Northcote Auckland 0627 New Zealand
86 Edgware Road London W2 2EA United Kingdom
80 McKenzie Street Cape Town 8001 South Africa

10 9 8 7 6 5 4 3 2 1 / 2 4 6 8 10 9 7 5 3 1National Library of
Australia Cataloguing-in-Publication Data:

Ferrett, Russell Richard.
        Earthquakes and volcanoes.

        Bibliography.
        Includes index.
        For primary school age.
        ISBN 9781921073359 (hbk.).

        1. Earthquakes - Juvenile literature. 2. Volcanoes -
Juvenile literature. I. Title.

        551.2

Commissioning Editor: Yani Silvana
Designer: Tania Gomes
Production: Linda Bottari
Printer: Tien Wah Press, Malaysia

Picture credits

JD Griggs, USGS Hawaiian Volcano Observatory:
    page 3 and 21, 32
Scott Ferrett: Marine Iguana page 17, Osorno page 17 and 23

When the Earth Moves

Earthquakes and Volcanoes

Russell Ferrett

Contents

All About Earth

Scientists are yet to find signs of life on any planet other than Earth. 'What makes the Earth so special?' you might ask. Three things: a solid crust, air and water.

Air to Breathe

Our Earth has oxygen in its **atmosphere** and this allows us and other animals to breathe.

A Solid Crust

The Earth has a solid **crust** made of rock. Some of the other planets, especially the really big ones, are giant balls of gas. The rocky surface is important: rocks break down to form soil, and soil allows trees, grass and other plants to grow. Once you have plants, animals like insects, birds and mammals have something to eat.

Crust, but not Toast

The Earth's crust is thin compared with the **mantle** and the **core**. The distance from the centre of the Earth to the outer edge of the core is 3500 kilometres. From the outer edge of the core through the mantle to the bottom of the crust is around 2850 kilometres. The crust, however, is not exactly solid. It's like a round hard-boiled egg that has been dropped and its shell has cracked into small pieces.

Water, Water, Everywhere

The Earth has just the right temperature for water to exist as a liquid, a solid and a gas. Rivers and ocean are made up of liquid water. Snow and ice at the tops of mountains and around the north and south poles are solid water. And water exists as a gas in the air as water vapour. Water vapour is invisible, but when it condenses it makes clouds, fog and rain. We and other animals need water to drink, plants need it to grow and fish need it to live in.

Earth's Structure

1. The **core** is made up mainly of the metals iron and nickel. It is partly solid and partly liquid.
2. The **mantle** is a mixture of different types of rocky material not quite hot enough to be **molten** and not quite cool enough to be solid. The mantle is classified as a liquid, but it is thicker than toothpaste, more like plasticine or play-dough.
3. The **crust** is a thin, relatively solid rocky layer that 'floats' on the mantle. The crust is thinnest under the oceans, where it is 6–10 kilometres thick. The continents are made up of lighter rock and

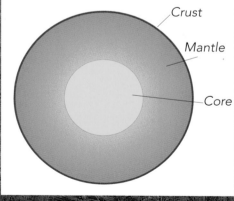

Crust

Mantle

Core

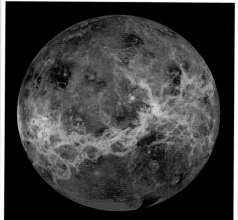

Earth versus Venus and Mars

How different are we from our neighbour planets, Venus and Mars? Venus is about the same size as Earth, but it is much hotter because it is closer to the Sun. It has an **atmosphere** of greenhouse gasses and droplets of acid. There is no water on Venus. Temperatures on the surface of Venus are often higher than 450°C. How hot is it at your place to day?

Mars is further away from the Sun than Earth and has very little atmosphere. Temperatures are constantly below zero on most of the planet. Some places are colder than −100°C. There is no water so it is very dry; strong winds create huge **dust** storms that blow for months on end.

Volcanoes on Venus?

Do other planets have volcanoes? Yes. Venus has many. The largest, Maat Mons, is 8000 metres high with a near-circular central crater 30 kilometres across. Mars has an even bigger one, Olympus Mons, the biggest volcano in the whole Solar System. It is 27 kilometres high and has a crater 81 kilometres across. Mona Loa, Hawaii, the largest volcano on Earth, rises 10,200 metres above the sea floor and has a crater that is 5 kilometres x 3 kilometres wide.

Earthquakes on Mars?

Do other planets have earthquakes? We don't know yet, but almost certainly. Those with solid crusts like Mercury, Venus and Mars have all formed in the same manner as Earth, so they probably do have earthquakes. To find out if they have earthquakes, scientists are placing measuring instruments on their surfaces. Perhaps we shouldn't use the word 'earthquakes' when referring to these other planets, but say mercuryquakes, venusquakes or marsquakes?

Pangea, Plates and Mountains

The Earth's **crust** is broken into large pieces called plates. The largest plate lies under the Pacific Ocean. The other larger plates each contain a continent. How many continental plates can you find on the world map?

Parting Plates

It may be hard to imagine, but the Earth's **crustal plates** move very, very slowly. About 250 million years ago all of today's continents were joined together into one large super-continent scientists call Pangea. After that time Pangea began to split up and the continents began drifting away from one another. If you look closely at the map (right) you can see how South America, if it were moved to the east, would sit nicely next to Africa, and North America and Greenland would fit well against Europe. At the time Pangea existed there was no Atlantic Ocean.

North American Plate

Caribbean Plate

Cocos Plate

Pacific Plate

Nazca Plate

South American Plate

Eurasian Plate

Arabian Plate

African Plate

Pacific Plate

Philippine Plate

Indo-Australian Plate

Antarctic Plate

N

0   5000
Kilometres

Hot Soup

Why do the crustal plates move? Because the thick liquid **mantle** on which they float moves beneath them. Have you ever watched soup boiling in a pot on the stove? Notice that even before the soup reaches boiling point the surface begins to move. This is because the soup at the bottom of the pot is heated by the hot plate. The hot soup rises to the top and colder soup from the top sinks to the bottom. This type of movement is called a **convection current**.

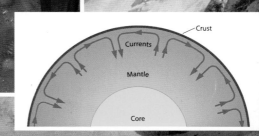

Crust

Currents

Mantle

Core

The Earth's core, at about 7000°C, is the hottest place in the Earth. The core heats the bottom of the mantle, setting up convection currents just like the soup in a pot. The hot mantle rises towards the surface and the cooler mantle sinks towards the core. This movement is very slow as

Crustal Collisions

A different type of crustal plate collision occurs when a heavy under-ocean plate crashes into a lighter continental plate. Along the western edge of the Pacific Ocean the Pacific Plate's western movement is causing it to collide with Japan, Indonesia, New Guinea, New Zealand and other countries. When a heavy plate pushes against a lighter plate, the pushing edge of the heavier one turns down under the lighter plate. The heavy plate sinks down into the **mantle** where it gets hotter and begins to melt, forming new **magma**. The movement of one plate down beneath another is called **subduction**.

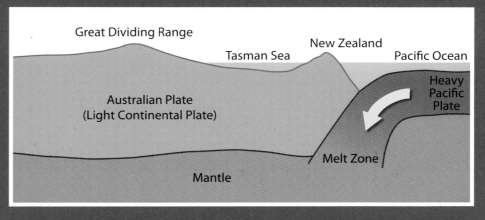

Making Mountains

Drifting continents sometimes crash into one another. Like cars crashing together, this causes damage. One of the most common forms of damage is for the edges of the colliding continents to crinkle. Geologists refer to crinkling as **folding**. For example, the Himalayan Mountains, which contain the world's highest mountain, Mount Everest, were formed when the Indian Plate crashed into the Eurasian Plate. Unlike cars, which usually stop quickly after a collision, **crustal plates** keep going, sometimes for millions of years. India, at the western end of the Indo-Australian Plate, is still pushing north against Asia, so Mount Everest and the Himalayas are

Earth-shattering
Earthquakes

An earthquake is the shaking of part of the Earth's **crust**. Earthquakes occur along the plate boundaries every time a plate buckles a little more, or slides further beneath another plate (subducts), or one plate slides along the side of another. Sometimes there are also earthquakes along faults—breaks in the Earth's crust away from plate boundaries. Pressure from below will cause rock on one side of a **fault** to rise or fall in relation to rock on the other side of the fault, causing the area near it to shake.

Look carefully at the map below and then at the map on page 8. Can you see that parts of them are very similar? Notice how the major earthquake zones are close to the boundaries between the plates. Look for some of the smaller earthquake zones away from the plate boundaries.

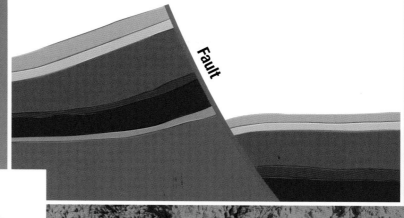

Fault

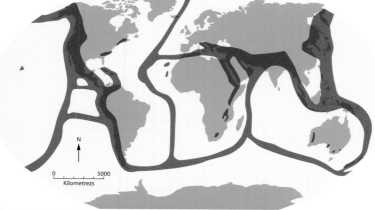

Shattered Rocks

Although lines on a map showing faults and plate boundaries are thin, the actual faults and the plate boundaries can be quite wide. Even a small **fault** like the one in the Little Bighorn Mountains of America is more than 200 metres wide. The rock on each side of the fault has been shattered into large blocks. At the edge of plates where **subduction** occurs, the zone of

The Richter Scale

After an earthquake has occurred we all want to know just how big it was. Back in 1935 Charles Richter, an American scientist, developed a scale to measure earthquakes. The scale goes from 0 for no earthquake up to 10 or more for massive quakes.

Scale	Effect
1	Not felt.
2	Normally not felt.
3	Generally not felt but recorded by instruments.
4	Normally felt, but causes little or no damage.
5	Shaking of furniture and ground vibration, but no significant structural damage.
6	Major damage to poorly constructed buildings, with some loss of life.
7	Serious damage up to 240 kilometres from its centre, with great loss of life in densely settled areas if people live in poorly constructed buildings. Some bridges and overpasses may collapse.
8	Mass destruction of buildings, failure of transport systems and great loss of life over a large area.
9	Devastation over a wide area; in densely settled regions many thousands of people could die.
10	Unknown. A scale 10 earthquake has never been recorded.

From Los Angeles to San Francisco

The part of California, USA, on which Los Angeles is built is moving north along the San Andreas Fault at an average rate of 3–4 centimetres a year. If you wait for 30 million years to make this journey, the distance between the two cities should have shrunk from around 1000 kilometres to less than 50. There have been lots of earthquakes along the San Andreas Fault, often causing destruction in cities like San Francisco and Los Angeles. The background picture shows the 'Fault Gouge' in the Southern California desert, which is a **solidified** mud-like substance squeezed up from beneath the surface by the grinding and moving pressure of the Earth's plates.

Measuring Earthquakes

Earthquakes are measured using a machine called a **seismograph**. Seismographs consist of a round drum covered by graph paper and a pen mounted on a long arm. When an earthquake occurs the pen moves up and down with the shaking. The more violent the shaking, the longer the lines drawn by the machine. Some seismographs are so accurate and sensitive that they can measure earthquakes that occur on the other side of the world.

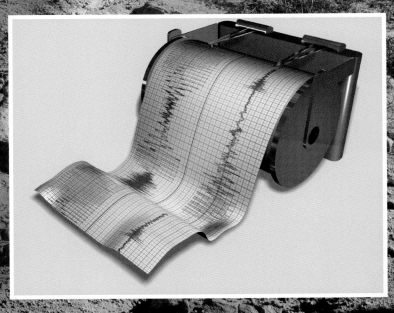

Earthquake
Disasters

Earthquakes can cause a lot of death and destruction. Collapsing buildings, and fires started by fuel stoves and fallen electricity wires, cause most deaths and injuries. Unlike volcanoes, which may rumble and smoke for months before a major eruption, there are no warning signs for earthquakes. More people get hurt in areas where a lot of people live close together, and where buildings are constructed from stone, mud-brick and non-reinforced concrete, which can less easily resist the force of the earthquake.

Turkey's Night of Terror

Izmit, Turkey, 3.02 am 17 August 1999. With the first jolt lights went out. Buildings shook. Sirens blared. Choking **dust** filled the air. Sleeping people woke screaming. Terrified, many ran for the safety of open space. For a very long 48 seconds, the earth shook violently. Then, relative peace. The shaking stopped. People called to one another in the dark. Some were crying. Light appeared in the sky. Street lights were coming back on? No. The massive oil refinery was alight. In the morning 17,000 were dead, 24,000 were injured, 120,000 homes were destroyed. The magnitude 7.6 earthquake was the eleventh to strike along this **fault** since 1939.

Aftershock!

Aftershocks are smaller earthquakes triggered by a large earthquake. The large earthquake shakes an area so violently that it causes movement along nearby faults. The 2005 Pakistani earthquake triggered more than 100 aftershocks within 24 hours of its occurrence.

Newcastle Shakes

At 10.30am on 28 December 1989 a 5.6 scale earthquake struck Newcastle, a city of around 300,000 people just north of Sydney, Australia. Normally an earthquake this size causes little damage, but not so in Newcastle. A number of buildings collapsed; nine people were killed in one. A further three were crushed by awnings that fell to the street in a suburban shopping centre. Another person died from a heart attack.

Disaster in Kashmir

On 8 October 2005 the earth shook in an isolated, but densely populated part of Kashmir. This was near where the Indo-Australian Plate pushes up against the Eurasian Plate. About 75,000 people died, mostly because of buildings collapsing. Broken bridges and phone lines made it hard to get help, especially in outlying farm communities.

Big Earthquakes on Record

Year	Place	Size	Deaths
1556	Shaanxi, China	8.0	830,000
1906	San Francisco, USA	7.8	3000
1923	Tokyo, Japan	7.9	143,000
1941	Meeberrie, Western Australia	7.2	0
1960	Valdiva, Chile	9.5	5700
1964	Anchorage, Alaska USA	8.5	125
1976	Tangshan, China	7.5	400,000
1989	Newcastle, New South Wales, Australia	5.6	13
1999	Izmit, Turkey	7.6	17,118
2004	Off Sumatra, Indonesia	9.3	230,000
2005	Kashmir, Pakistan	7.6	75,000

Afghanistan Grows Higher Every Day

Afghanistan and parts of Pakistan experience, on average, two major earthquakes per year. The region is caught between two colliding giants, the Eurasian Plate to the north and the Indo-Australian Plate to the south. These plates are coming together at 30 to 40 centimetres a year, causing this part of the Earth's **crust** to buckle upwards. (Australia is moving north at only 6–8 centimetres per year and is considered to be a 'fast mover'.) As much of the land is dry, there are few trees to provide timber to build houses. Many homes are built of stone—they collapse when struck by nearby earthquakes.

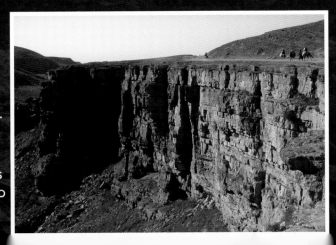

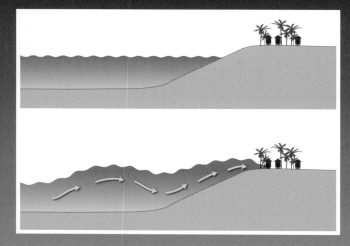

Huge Waves

Ships at sea barely notice **tsunamis**. The water around the ships gently lifts a small amount, normally less than a metre, and then equally gently settles down. The change would be no more noticeable than that from the normal waves at sea. But as tsunamis approach land the waves are slowed down by their contact with the ocean floor. The shockwaves bend upwards forcing the surface of the water to rise rapidly as it moves forward. An approaching tsunami wave can be more than 30 metres high and wash inland for several kilometres.

Boxing Day Tsunami

On 26 December 2004 a huge tsunami struck countries around the Indian Ocean. It was caused by an earthquake off the west coast of the island of Sumatra in Indonesia. This earthquake registered 9.3 on the Richter Scale, the second largest ever recorded. It extended along a **fault** line 1600 kilometres long, the longest ever recorded. The quake started at the southern end of the fault, near Sumatra, then spread northwards before reaching its end ten minutes later. Ten minutes is an incredibly long period for the violent shaking of an earthquake. Thousands of people died. In places the seabed was lifted 5 metres and shifted sideways a further 10–15 metres. Some new islands even appeared out of what had been shallow sea before the quake.

From its centre the tsunami spread out in all directions till it reached land. It took only 15 minutes to reach Sumatra's beaches, but one and a half hours to reach Sri Lanka, two hours to India and Thailand, seven hours to Somalia and 16 hours to South Africa.

No April Fool's Joke

Just after 1am on 1 April 1946 a 14 metre tsunami swept into Hilo, a city on the island of Hawaii. The tsunami had originated from a magnitude 7.2 earthquake five hours earlier in the Aleutian Islands off the coast of Alaska. Seven separate crests, each about 15 minutes apart, crashed into and wiped out every house along the city's main street that ran parallel to the harbour shore. One hundred and fifty-nine people died and 1300 homes were destroyed.

A Repeat Performance

Hilo suffered a second devastating tsunami in 1960 following the world's largest earthquake in modern times. The earthquake, off the coast of Chile, had a magnitude of 9.5. The tsunami took 15 hours to reach the city. Sixty-one people died. The Pacific Tsunami Warning Center in Hawaii was created as a result of Hilo's two major disasters. It provides tsunami warnings for all countries bordering the Pacific Ocean. The waterfront in

Terrifying Tsunamis

Tsunamis are giant waves caused by powerful underwater events such as earthquakes, volcanic eruptions and landslides. These events create a shockwave that passes through the water at up to 800 kilometres per hour. The word tsunami (soo-nahm-ee) comes from two Japanese words; tsu meaning harbour and nami meaning wave. Tsunamis are common in Japan, where many earthquakes occur close to and in the ocean around the islands. Tsunamis are most dangerous in the funnel-shaped harbours common in Japan because the force of the advancing water becomes focused at the end of the harbour.

A Suffering Country

Japan averages at least one bad tsunami every decade. Children at school have regular earthquake and tsunami survival drills. Loudspeaker systems warn the people in towns and villages. Large concrete barriers have been built along the coast in some areas to protect them from small to medium tsunamis. But in 1993, these systems were not enough to protect the small island of Okushiri. Two minutes after the island was shaken by a 7.8 magnitude earthquake, the first of 13 waves struck. The largest was 30 metres high. There was no time for warnings, but many people were saved by running to higher ground. Still, 197 were drowned. Could you get out of bed and run to the top of the closest hill in two minutes?

Volcanoes
around the World

There are **active** or **dormant** volcanoes on every continent, on hundreds of islands and even under the sea. Volcanic areas have fertile soil, so many people are drawn to live near volcanoes, even the active ones, where it's easy to grow food.

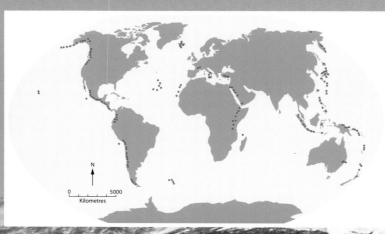

Look carefully at the map to the left and then the maps on pages 8 and 10. Can you see that many parts are similar? Notice how the main volcanic areas follow the same plate boundaries, as do the earthquake zones. Both earthquakes and volcanoes are found along lines of weakness in the crust. The lines along which plates touch one another are major lines of weakness.

Hawaiian Volcanoes

The largest volcanic mountain in the world is the Big Island of Hawaii. The volcano at the centre of the island stands nearly 4200 metres above sea level, but its base is down a further 6000 metres on the floor of the Pacific Ocean. Kilauea, an **active volcano** on the side of the Big Island has been erupting almost continually since 1983. Other volcanoes on the Big Island **erupt** less frequently; during quieter periods the surface **lava** in these craters crusts over as it cools.

© Simon Goldsworthy

Big Ben

Big Ben is an active volcano located in the Australian Territory of Heard Island in the Great Southern Ocean, close to Antarctica. It is 2745 metres high and 20 kilometres across at the base. At the top is a deep crater that is 5 kilometres wide. Big Ben erupts every one or two years. Being close to Antarctica, the sides of the volcano are covered with ice and snow that in places reach right down to the ocean.

Mount Etna

The largest volcano in Europe, Mount Etna, has been **erupting** almost continuously for hundreds of years. During its life, which began nearly 500,000 years ago, it has built a shield cone 60 x 40 kilometres wide and 2900 metres high. **Magma** beneath Mount Etna contains large quantities of carbon dioxide, so **fountaining** is common. Many tourists come to view the spectacular displays. **Lava-flows** sometimes more than 10 kilometres long have, over time, destroyed many villages, but taken few lives. Large concrete barriers have been built to divert future lava-flows around some of the towns built on the sides of the volcano.

Mt Etna

Osorno, a volcano in Chile, South America

Galapagos Islands

The isolated Galapagos Islands, 1000 kilometres off the west coast of South America, were formed from volcanic eruptions. Charles Darwin, a scientist, visited these islands and used the unusual animal life found here in developing his theory of evolution. The unusual Marine Iguanas that live on these islands are vegetarian and are thought to have evolved to eat seaweed due to a shortage of normal land-based vegetation growing on the rocky surface of the islands.

Collapsed Volcano

Sometimes a volcano will collapse, forming what is called a **caldera**. The world's largest collapsed volcano is Ngorongoro in Tanzania, Africa. Around 8 million years ago, it stopped erupting—the **lava** suddenly stopped flowing. The lava left in the crater began to sink back into the hole beneath the volcano and the top of the volcano collapsed back into the hole, partly filling it. All that remains is a caldera 20 kilometres wide and 600 metres deep. Within the caldera, lush tropical grass grows in the rich volcanic soil, attracting 25,000 large animals such as lions, giraffes, buffalo, deer and wildebeest—perhaps the world's largest zoo!

What is a **Volcano?**

Volcanoes are places where **molten** rock from below the Earth's **crust** rises to the surface. Some volcanoes build high mountains, while the **lava** from others flows over the surface to produce plains. Some volcanoes explode; in others, molten rock flows out of a hole as if from a giant **pipe**. Some **erupt** once and then die; others live and erupt for millions of years. Some have a simple round hole at the top; others are cracks hundreds of kilometres long. The most common volcano shape on land is a cone. Did you know that there are also many volcanoes under the sea?

Too Hot to Handle

Rock at the centre of the earth is hot. Very, very hot. Somewhere between 5000 and 7000°C. Most rock has a melting point of between 1000 and 1500°C. If you were to dig a hole towards the centre of the Earth, the temperature would rise, on average, by 30°C for every kilometre you dug down. By the time you reached a depth of 35 kilometres the rocks around you would have started to melt. This is where the **molten** rock that is brought to the surface by volcanoes comes from.

Plume Volcanoes

The Earth's **core** is continually churning and twisting around, giving off huge amounts of heat. Sometimes a burst of super heat from the core travels to the surface. These pockets of rising heat are called plumes. Pressure and heat from the rising plume can melt the **crust** above the plume, allowing the magma to flow out at the surface as a plume volcano. Plume volcanoes tend to be cone-shaped, but not as steep as subduction volcanoes.

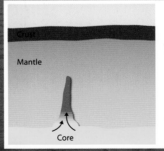
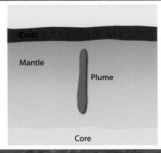
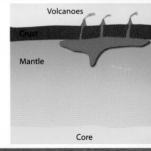

Hotspot Volcanoes

Sometimes a burst of super heat from the core (see 'Plume Volcanoes' on page 24) continues for tens of millions of years. This continuous stream of heat creates a **hot spot** on the surface. Hot-spot volcanoes **erupt** for millions of years before eventually dying when the burst of super heat ends. They are the same shape as plume volcanoes.

Subduction Volcanoes

Where two **crustal plates** collide, the heavier one sinks down into the **mantle** and the lighter one rides up over the other plate. This downward movement of the heavy plate is called **subduction**. The front of the heavy plate melts and forms new **magma**. As the heavy plate sinks lower and lower into the mantle, the newly formed magma gets squeezed up through cracks in the lighter plate above, and erupts on the surface as a subduction volcano.

Fissure Volcanoes

If subduction volcanoes form when two crustal plates collide, what happens if two plates separate by pulling apart? A large crack, called a fissure, grows. The fissure becomes wider and wider as the two plates drift further and further apart. But before the fissure gets more than a couple of metres wide, magma rises up to weld the plates back together again. As the plates continue separating, the welds break, only to be filled again with magma. This breaking and welding can go on for hundreds of millions of years. Fissure volcanoes can be thousands of kilometres long, but usually only shorter sections are active at any one time.

Is it Magma or is it Lava?

Molten rock beneath the surface is called magma. Once it flows out of the volcano it's called lava. Most lava has a temperature of 1000 to 1200°C as it flows from a volcano.

Lava Lakes

Lava pouring from a non-explosive volcano tends to flow away and downhill from its **vent** (opening). Hot lava melts the rock at the sides of the vent, making the hole larger. When the lava stops flowing, the vent will remain full of **molten**, boiling lava for weeks, or even months—a **lava lake**. Anyone for a swim? Eventually the lava cools and becomes solid.

To Explode or not to Explode

Not all volcanoes explode. The ones that do are called subduction volcanoes. But what causes them to explode? The answer to this question may surprise you: water and carbon dioxide **gas**. About one two-hundredth of the weight of most **lava** coming out of a volcano is water and carbon dioxide. Another way of saying this is, in every 200 tonnes of lava, there is 1 tonne of water and gas. That may not sound much, but it can have a very explosive effect.

Fountains of Lava

Some volcanoes spurt out glowing fountains of **lava** that can be more than 100 metres high. This happens when rapidly escaping carbon dioxide **gas** from very liquid, very hot lava, throws droplets of lava and **lava froth** high into the air. **Fountaining** is spectacular, especially at night, and may continue for several weeks.

A Steamy Explosion

Some lava contains water as well as **gas**—for example the lava of volcanoes located near where ocean plates subduct beneath continental plates. Trapped within the rocks, this boiling hot water cannot turn to steam. But as the **magma** moves closer to the surface the pressure drops, and steam explodes out of the volcano—a litre of water can turn into 2000 litres of steam in an instant. If there is enough water in the lava, it can blow the volcano to bits.

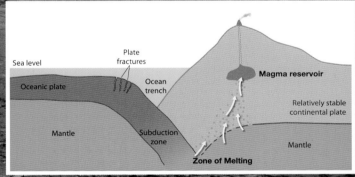

Water from Where?

If explosive volcanoes are the ones that contain water in their magma, where does the water come from? When plates subduct under the sea, water is carried in cracks in the rock down to the top of the **mantle**. When the rock eventually melts, the rising magma carries the water back towards the surface.

Non-exploding Volcanoes

Volcanoes with no water don't explode. About half the volcanoes on dry land contain no water. They tend to **erupt** when pressure from below forces magma to the surface. This pressure can be sufficient to break the rock above the rising magma, but does not blast it into the air. The lava flows out through the holes or cracks in the rock. The volcanoes in Hawaii and Iceland are of this type as were the now **extinct/dormant** volcanoes in Australia.

Subduction Volcanoes

Subduction volcanoes are the very explosive ones. You sometimes see them on the TV news, causing death and destruction. They are found close to the sea at the edge of continental plates, above subducting ocean floor plates.

Froth and Bubble

With all the churning from rising **gas**, exploding steam and gushing **magma** from deep below, **lava** on the surface becomes frothy just like the froth on a milkshake. **Lava froth** is air and other gas trapped in bubbles of **molten** rock. As the froth cools, the casing of lava becomes solid. Lava froth is remarkably light, but it is also fragile and easily broken. When a volcano erupts, the froth is thrown into the **atmosphere** and shatters into small fragments called **ash**, cinder or **scoria**.

Building Cones

When a volcano erupts it throws out a lot of volcanic froth and droplets of **lava**. These fall to the ground around the volcano's opening, or **vent**, building a steep cone. Most subduction volcanoes build cones with alternating layers of lava and volcanic **cinder**. These are called **composite cones**. You have probably built small cones by letting dry sand pour through your cupped hands. Volcanoes build cones in the same way but they throw their building material up into the air before it falls to the ground. Later, flows of lava cover the pebbly material, holding it together. The volcano grows bigger and bigger as this process is repeated.

Ash and cinder

Lava

Magma reservoir

The Pacific Ring of Fire

Most of the world's violent volcanoes are on what is known as 'The Pacific Ring of Fire'. This line of subduction volcanoes surrounds the Pacific Ocean on three sides—the west, north and east. The volcanoes are there because of the movement of the Pacific crustal plate and the continental plates that surround it. North and South America are pushing westward, the Pacific Plate is pushing under New Zealand, New Guinea, Japan and Alaska and the Australian Plate is pushing north against Indonesia.

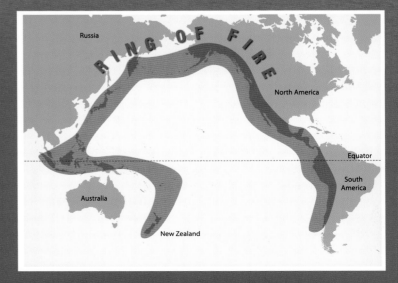

Osorno

Osorno, a volcano in Chile, South America, erupted 11 times between 1575 and 1869. It had, of course, erupted many times before this, but no records were made of these eruptions. It last erupted in 1869 so an eruption is long overdue.

Over and Over Again

Many volcanoes, particularly subduction ones, **erupt** again and again, with many years between each eruption. When a volcano erupts it releases all the pressure that has built up prior to the eruption. It does not erupt again till pressure has again rebuilt. Pressure build up in subduction volcanoes comes from that very slow downward movement as oceanic **crustal plates** subduct. As the crustal movement is slow, the creation of new **magma** and the build up of pressure is equally slow.

A Smelly Volcano

Ngauruhoe (Nu-ra-hoe-ee) in New Zealand is a good example of a subduction volcano that has developed a steep composite cone. This volcano is still active and growing. Inside the volcano you can see the different layers of **ash** and **cinder**. Smoke and steam smelling of rotten egg gas rises from the bottom of the crater, which is coated with sulphur. Imagine what it would be like to walk along the trail that runs around the crater rim.

Plume and Hotspot Volcanoes

Plume and **hotspot volcanoes** are really the same; it's just that plumes have a relatively short life and hot spots last for millions of years. Plume and hotspot volcanoes don't explode. Like subduction volcanoes, plume and hotspot volcanoes build cones, but they are much flatter. Some are so flat that they are called shield volcanoes—they look like an ancient foot soldier's shield lying on the ground. Mount Warning, an **extinct** volcano in New South Wales, Australia, was 2 kilometres high, but 100 kilometres wide at its base.

Plume Volcanoes

In Australia, only a few thousand years ago, there were active plume volcanoes in northern Queensland, and in western Victoria and into South Australia. Although these volcanoes are not active today, the plumes that created them are still there and volcanoes could again **erupt** in these regions. More than 150 old volcanoes have been found on the Atherton Tableland in Queensland, but most are small.

Lava Tubes

Sometimes the surface of flowing **lava** cools and crusts over, while hot molten lava continues to flow beneath. Such places are called **lava tubes**. The more lava flows, the longer the tube gets. When the volcano stops erupting and the lava stops flowing, the tubes become empty tunnels. Lava tubes are commonly found on the sides of plume and **hotspot volcanoes**.

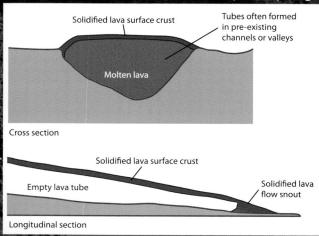

Solidified lava surface crust

Tubes often formed in pre-existing channels or valleys

Molten lava

Cross section

Solidified lava surface crust

Empty lava tube

Solidified lava flow snout

Longitudinal section

The Longest Lava Tubes

An extraordinary **lava-flow** occurred at Undara just to the south of the Atherton Tableland in Queensland about 190,000 years ago. The eruption lasted just three months and in that short time 23 cubic kilometres of lava flowed from its crater. That is enough lava to fill Sydney Harbour more than 40 times. Most of the **molten** rock flowed through two lava tubes (tunnels), one 160 kilometres long, and the other 100 kilometres long. The lava tubes at Undara are the longest in the world.

Hawaiian Hot Spots

You would think that all **hotspot volcanoes** would grow huge due to their continuous supply of lava, but this is not so. Hot spots are fixed to the Earth's **core**, but the **crustal plates** (see page 18) above them are continually on the move. The Hawaiian Islands have been formed by a single **hot spot** rising beneath the Pacific plate. The Pacific plate is moving slowly to the north-west over the stationary hot spot, forming a chain of volcanoes running in line from the north-west to the south-east. The oldest volcano, Kauai is in the north-west, with Oahu next, then Molokai and Maui, followed by Hawaii, the largest and youngest, in the south-east.

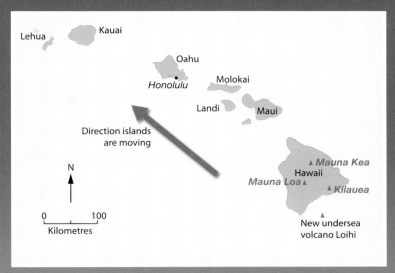

Lava, Lava and More Lava

Although the Hawaiian volcanoes have erupted great quantities of **ash** and **cinder** by **fountaining**, they are best known for their spectacular **lava-flows**. Kilauea, on the Big Island of Hawaii, has been erupting a near continuous stream of lava since 1983. Lava is flowing from large cracks on the side of the mountain and flowing down to the ocean.

Bright Red Rivers

Large flows of lava look like bright red rivers tumbling down the mountainside. But these are not the type of river you would like to swim in. Their temperatures are around 1000°C. Once the lava reaches the plain its speed slows, the lava spreads out, and it turns a bright shiny black as the surface cools and becomes solid rock.

Slow and Steady

Do you think that the lava was breaking the speed limit as it flowed along this road? No. When the lava reached this point it was much cooler than when it started higher up the mountain and the land over which it is flowing is quite flat. The lava probably crossed the road at less than 1 kilometre per hour. You could walk faster than that.

When Lava Meets the Sea

Does this photo show another volcanic eruption close to the edge of the island? No. It's just where lava from further up on the mountain is running down and into the sea. That is not smoke rising from the water. It is steam.

Australia's Hotspot Volcanoes

Australia has a chain of **hotspot volcanoes** that is even older than the chain in Hawaii, but none of these are active today.

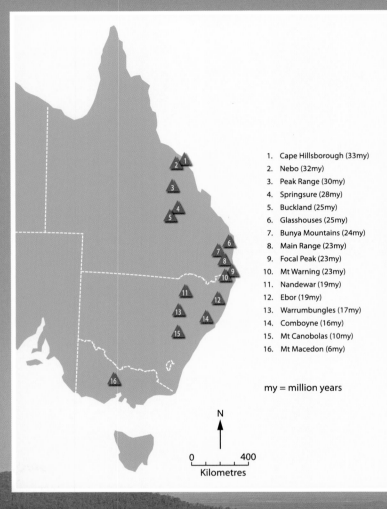

1. Cape Hillsborough (33my)
2. Nebo (32my)
3. Peak Range (30my)
4. Springsure (28my)
5. Buckland (25my)
6. Glasshouses (25my)
7. Bunya Mountains (24my)
8. Main Range (23my)
9. Focal Peak (23my)
10. Mt Warning (23my)
11. Nandewar (19my)
12. Ebor (19my)
13. Warrumbungles (17my)
14. Comboyne (16my)
15. Mt Canobolas (10my)
16. Mt Macedon (6my)

my = million years

N

0 ————— 400
Kilometres

A Wobbly Chain

Australia has been moving north at the rate of 8 centimetres a year for millions of years. That's about the rate your fingernails grow. But the hot spot coming from the Earth's **core** is staying in the same place. So we have a wobbly line of **extinct** (dead) volcanoes stretching from Cape Hillsborough in the north, to near Mount Macedon, close to Melbourne, in the south. The hot spot is also wide, so some volcanoes, particularly in New South Wales, are in pairs, side by side.

The oldest in Australia's chain of hotspot volcanoes is at Cape Hillsborough on the central coast of Queensland. It first erupted 33 million years ago, but probably died within one million years before reappearing at Nebo.

Flows and Waterfalls

Some volcanoes produce a huge amount of **lava** that flows for many kilometres and may be hundreds of metres thick. The Ebor Volcano (look for it on the map) was one such volcano. This volcano has been **extinct** for 19 million years, but when it was active it produced **lava-flows** up to 50 kilometres long. After several million years of erupting and resting the volcano's lava-flows were thick enough to fill all the valleys and cover all the hills around it. Rivers flowing over the old lava-flows develop waterfalls as they cut into the rock.

Can you see the three different lava-flows in this picture of the Upper Ebor Falls? There are two different flows in the larger fall and one just below it.

A Spooky Place

Hanging Rock on the side of Mount Macedon in Victoria is the youngest and furthest south of Australia's hotspot volcanoes. Mount Macedon itself is not part of the line of hotspot volcanoes; it is almost 400 million years old. Hanging Rock is much younger—only 6 million years old. The top of Hanging Rock is made of rock towers up to 20 metres high, separated by narrow canyons wide enough for spooky dark paths and tracks to wind between them. Have you read the book *Picnic at Hanging Rock* or seen the film?

Pyramids in Queensland

The Glasshouse Mountains in Queensland look like lots of Egypt's pyramids set in a green field. They formed 25 million years ago, when the **hot spot** was beneath them. We do not know which is the oldest, or youngest, or the order in which they were formed. The first one grew as a volcano. When that volcano stopped erupting, the lava in it became solid. So when it tried to **erupt** again, it had to find a new way to the surface, so it grew a new volcano. This happened over and over till there were 13 volcanoes all close together.

Maars, Geysers
and Boiling Pools

Maars, geysers and boiling pools of water and mud all look different from one another, but have one thing in common: they form where **magma** heats water under the ground. This happens in areas of high rainfall where there are plumes beneath the surface, as in New Zealand and Yellowstone in the USA, or where water is carried beneath the surface in limestone caves, as in parts of Victoria.

What is a Maar?

A **maar** is a type of plume volcano that forms when rising **magma** comes in contact with ground water just below the surface. When the magma reaches the water, the water gets hot and bursts into steam, blasting away the overlying rock. The resulting hole fills with water, forming a lake. Sometimes more magma reaches the surface later, and **lava** flows out forming a volcanic cone in the middle of the lake. Australia has more maars than any other country in the world.

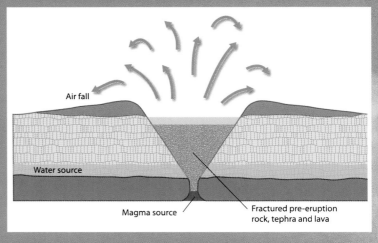

Air fall

Water source

Magma source

Fractured pre-eruption rock, tephra and lava

Not a Hill, But a Maar

Tower Hill, near Warrnambool, Victoria, is a maar. When rising magma came in contact with water in the underlying limestone rock, a hole 2 kilometres wide was blasted in the rock. Water filled the hole. Later, some eruptions formed a small volcano in the middle of the lake.

*Most of the eruptions at Tower Hill spewed out **ash** and **cinder**. You can see the horizontal layers of ash in a road cutting as you come through the entrance into the nature reserve.*

Blasting a Hole

At the top of Mount Hypipamee in Queensland is a huge hole. Its vertical sides are solid granite. At the bottom is a deep lake, green with algae. The lake is 87 metres deep and the walls above the waterline rise a further 55 metres. The hole is 60 metres wide. It was formed when rising magma heated the water trapped in the rock to hundreds of degrees and the rock cracked. Masses of steam exploded from the cracks, blowing out millions of tonnes of rock to create the Mount Hypipamee hole.

Hubble Bubble

Not all geysers **erupt**. Some just become small lakes of boiling water. There are several examples of these in Yellowstone National Park, USA.

'The Cauldron' in Yellowstone National Park, is about 10 metres across and 3 metres deep. It boils all day and all night even in winter when the park is covered by snow.

Sometimes chemicals in the water form colourful rings around a pool as the water evaporates.

This boiling mud pool near Rotorua in New Zealand is on a golf course. You wouldn't want to hit your golf ball into it, would you?

Boiling Mud

Some geysers form pools of boiling mud. They are similar to the boiling water geysers in Yellowstone National Park, USA, but because less steam and water flow from them and the surface is covered by soil rather than bare rock, they become pools of bubbling mud.

'Old Faithful' in Yellowstone National Park in the USA erupts every one and a half hours. Each eruption lasts for around two minutes. During that time 15,000–30,000 litres of water and steam are thrown 30–50 metres into the air.

Jets of Steam

Sometimes water trickling down through hot rocks gets so hot it turns to steam. The steam and water blast out at the surface through a natural **pipe** in the rock, creating what is called a **geyser**. After the water has been cleared from the pipe, more water runs in and the cycle starts again. Many geysers follow this pattern like clockwork.

Rift Volcanoes

You can't see many rift volcanoes because most of them, but not all, lie under the sea. In **geology**, a rift is a place where two parts of the Earth's **crust** are spreading apart, leaving a large crack.

Atlantic Rift

The best known **rift** lies in the middle of the Atlantic Ocean. The North and South American continents are moving west, away from Europe and Africa. A large crack in the **crust** runs the full length of the Atlantic from Iceland to Antarctica. The crack, however, does not stay open, but fills with lava that rises from the **mantle**. The lava quickly hardens into solid rock in the cold water and welds the gap closed. But as the rift continues to widen the crack reappears. Fresh lava pours into the crack and the crack is repaired again. This process of breaking and welding has been repeating for millions of years.

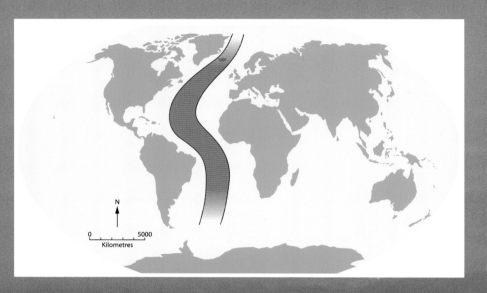

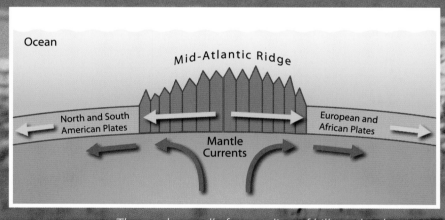

The crack actually forms a line of hills under the ocean, which is why it's called the Mid-Atlantic Ridge. When lava from the mantle rises to fill the gap it overflows and continues building up until enough of the lava is solidified by the cold sea water to block any further upwelling.

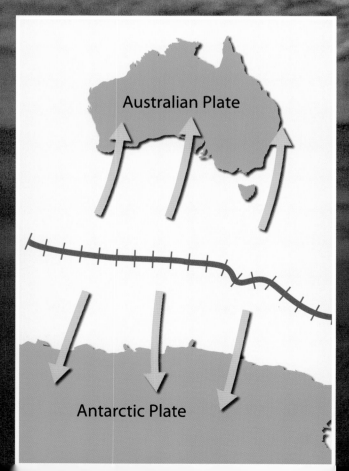

An Antarctic Rift

Another crack in the **crust** exists between Australia and Antarctica. With Australia's 8-centimetre-a-year drift to the north this gap is continually being stretched, broken, filled with **lava** and then stretched, broken and filled with lava. This has been happening for more than 50 million years.

Boiling Water Under the Sea?

Did you know that there are **geysers** under the sea? Boiling water and very hot gases escape from near the cracks in the **crust**. Chemicals carried by the hot water are deposited on the ocean floors, building up strange chimney towers around the geyser outlets. These towers are referred to as 'black smokers'. Scientists use special robot submarines to study the black smokers and the fish and other aquatic animals that live around them. The submarines are called submersibles and are used because the water is too deep to use normal submarines.

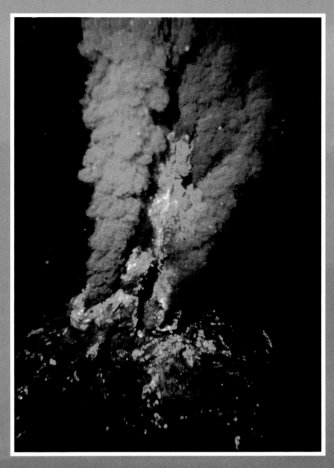

Underwater Canyons

These long cracks don't split open along their entire length at the same time. Instead, short sections break at different times. This causes the mid-ocean ridges to be broken by sharp underwater canyons that lie at right angles across the ridges

The floor of the Great Rift Valley in Africa is not perfectly flat. Lava-flows have made natural dams across it, forming swamps and lakes. Many of the lakes are called 'soda lakes' as they contain salt and volcanic impurities. The lakes are famous for their flamingos and other bird life.

Rifts on Land

Sometimes rifting happens on dry land. The best example is in Africa and marks the line along which part of Africa is slowly breaking away from the rest of the continent. The **rift** forms a great valley between the two sections, and is appropriately named The Great Rift Valley.

Like the cracks in the mid-ocean ridges, lava rises to fill the bottom of Africa's rift each time the crack opens. Lava-flows and small volcanic cones dot the valley floor.

Big Blocks

Blocks are solid pieces of rock torn away from the volcano's **pipe** as **lava**, **ash**, **cinder** and **gas** rush up to the surface. Small blocks are about the same size as lava **bombs**, but large blocks can weigh a tonne or more. The **maars** in Victoria (page 28) contain many blocks, as they were formed by eruptions exploding through limestone rock. When the blocks fall to Earth, they sink into the soft ash denting its neat horizontal layers.

Steep Cones

Most cinder falls close to the eruption site. Together with some ash, it will build steeply sloping cones. But these do not last long: cinder is easily moved by the wind or washed away by rain to form gentler slopes.

Ash and Stuff

Erupting subduction and plume volcanoes throw huge quantities of **lava** and broken rock into the air. All of this eventually falls to the ground, some much sooner than others. Vulcanologists call the stuff that falls to the ground following an eruption **'tephra'**.

Cinder

Cinder is bigger than ash; particles can be up to 6 centimetres across. Although it is quite light for its size, it is too heavy for the wind to blow it long distances. Cinder is usually black or grey when first erupted, but if it contains iron it will turn red after a few years. Red cinder is often called **scoria**.

You might have seen scoria used as mulch on garden beds.

Lava Bombs

Occasionally, escaping **gas** will blow large globs of molten lava into the air. As these globs pass through the air they cool quickly, forming a thin, solid **crust**. If the glob lands on soft **ash** it may survive its fall and stay intact. Such pieces of rock are called lava **bombs**. If you were standing near a volcano and a lava bomb hit you, it would kill you.

Splattered Rock

If **lava bomb**s fall on top of each other, they will splatter and build small cones just a few metres high and a few metres across. This accumulation of lava bombs is called **spatter**, and the resulting cones, spatter cones.

Pumice stone is used for removing thickened skin, especially from feet.

Bubble Rock

Pumice is similar to spatter, but is much lighter. As a volcano gently bubbles away it may develop a froth that floats on the surface like soap bubbles on bath water. Escaping gas from the **molten** lava may blow pieces of this froth into the air. It cools and hardens as it falls to the ground. Imagine a froth of soap bubbles made from rock. You could lift it with one finger. Pumice is often found close to spatter cones.

From Molten Lava to Rock

When **lava** flows from a volcano it runs downhill, as it is a liquid, and begins to cool because it is in contact with the air. Eventually it cools to a point where it becomes solid rock. Some **lava-flows** in parts of the north-western USA and southern India are hundreds of kilometres long and over 100 metres deep.

Black and Shiny

Fresh volcanic rock surfaces, which have formed from high temperature very liquid lava, are uneven, black and shiny. This type of surface is called pahoehoe (pah-hoy-hoy), a Hawaiian word meaning 'smooth'.

Ropes of Stone

Pahoehoe lava, also called **ropy lava**, may become crinkly on top as it cools. The surface of the lava touching the air cools to become like toffee, while the hotter lava beneath stays liquid and keeps flowing. This causes the surface to crinkle and twist so that it looks like large coils of rope laying on the surface.

Cracked!

As lava cools and solidifies, it develops fine cracks that run from the surface to the bottom of the flow. They are not visible at first, but over time, air and water enter these cracks causing them to get bigger.

When you look down on a lava-flow washed clean by a river you can clearly see the tops of these cracks. They look very much like cracks that develop in clay at the bottom of a dry dam.

Pencils in the Sky

If you look at the side of a **solidified lava-flow** it looks like a whole lot of rock columns fitted together like sticks of chalk in a box.

Columns at Mt Kaputar, New South Wales.

Rough and Broken

Aa (ah-ah) is a Hawaiian name given to rough volcanic rock surfaces formed from less hot thick, tacky lava. Slow-flowing lava churning over itself as it moves forward causes the broken and clinker-like surface to form.

Volcanic Rock

When lava cools and solidifies it forms volcanic rock. The most common volcanic rock is basalt, but there are others, including trachyte (track-ite) and obsidian. Differences between rock types occur because there are slight variations in their chemical composition.

Rocks that Rust

Basalt looks like any other dirty brown rock. But break it open and you'll see its true colour—a blue-grey. Basalt is a relatively soft rock, that's if you can ever call a rock soft. Under warm, wet conditions it quickly breaks down into soil. Geologists think that a million years is quick. When basalt breaks down, it turns into red soil. It is red because basalt contains some iron, and under warm wet conditions, iron rusts. The rust stains the soil red.

Honeycomb Rock

If the **gas** in lava comes out slowly as it does with an open bottle of fizzy soft drink, it leaves lots of little holes in the lava. When the lava has cooled to form solid rock, it looks like honeycomb. This rock is called **vesicular** rock, but you can just call it honeycomb rock.

Speckled Inside

Trachyte is a common volcanic rock in Australia. It is much harder than **basalt** and takes much longer to **erode** to form soil. The Glasshouse Mountains (Queensland), Mount Warning **plug**, the Warrumbungle plugs and **dykes** (New South Wales) and Hanging Rock (Victoria) are made of trachyte—that is why they have lasted so long. When broken open, trachyte is a speckled off-white colour.

Volcanic Glass

Obsidian, also known as volcanic glass, cools to form a rock that is shiny like glass. Unlike the clear glass in windows, obsidian is coloured—usually grey, brown and black. Obsidian is softer than basalt and can be carved into interesting shapes using special cutting tools attached to electric drills. You can sometimes find ornaments in gift shops made from obsidian.

Diamonds

Diamonds are not a volcanic rock, but they are carried to the surface by volcanoes. They form beneath the **crust** and, during an eruption, a rising plume or **hot spot** sometimes carries them to the surface. The world's largest diamond-producing mine is at Argyle in Western Australia, near the Northern Territory border. Diamonds were transported to the surface by a volcano that existed at Argyle 1200 million years ago.

Tuff But Not Tough

Tuff is made of compressed **ash** and **cinder**. When you say 'tuff' it sounds like a Londoner saying 'tough' (toof). The thing is, tuff is not very tough. People in some countries, for example Indonesia, carve tuff to make large ornaments and statues. But the best examples of this type of carving are found on Easter Island in the middle of the Southern Pacific Ocean. Hundreds of years ago, South Sea Island people carved giant heads out of tuff. They placed the heads along the coast with their backs to the sea so that they could watch over the people and keep away evil spirits. A head is called a 'moi' and a group of mois is called a 'choir'. But they can't sing can they?

Volcanic Disasters

Explosive volcanic eruptions often kill many people. Some of the worst disasters have occurred when island volcanoes have erupted, causing tsunamis. More than three-quarters of the deaths from the 1883 Krakatoa eruption in Indonesia, the world's second most deadly volcanic eruption, were from drownings on nearby islands.

Mount Tarawera, New Zealand

Mount Tarawera, New Zealand, erupted in 1886 when its **vent** became blocked by its own **lava**. Before the explosion, Mount Tarawera consisted of three peaks all in a line. First one peak erupted, then the other two exploded with equal violence. The force of the explosions was so great that the mountain split in two. One hundred and fifty Maori villagers were killed; any houses left standing were totally covered by falling ash.

Philippines Eruption

The eruption of Mount Pinatubo in the Philippines over a four-month period in 1991 was the world's largest eruption since the 1912 Novarupta erosion in Alaska. Mount Pinatubo is a subduction volcano on the Pacific Ring of Fire and had been **dormant** for 500 years. The eruption blasted 10 cubic kilometres of **tephra** into the air. Smoke and **ash** reached 34 kilometres in the air. Although early warnings of the eruption saved thousands of lives, at least 300 people were killed. Most died when buildings collapsed under the weight of ash that fell on their roofs.

Eruptions Around the World

This table lists some of the better known eruptions and the deaths they caused.
Many of the numbers given are estimates, as the exact number will never be known.

Volcano	Country	Year	Deaths
Tambora	Indonesia	1815	92,000
Krakatoa	Indonesia	1883	35,000
Mount Pelee	Martinique	1902	29,000
Unzen	Japan	1792	14,000
Vesuvius	Italy	1586	3500
Vesuvius	Italy	79	3300
Pinatubo	Philippines	1991	800
Tarawera	New Zealand	1886	150
Mount St Helens	USA	1980	57

Pompeii Destroyed

Although it happened almost 2000 years ago, the destruction of the Roman town of Pompeii by an eruption of Mount Vesuvius is still the best known volcanic disaster in history. In the early hours of 24 August 79 AD, when most people were asleep, Vesuvius erupted, covering the city with **ash**. Fortunately many residents had already left the city of 20,000 inhabitants because the volcano had been rumbling and blowing black smoke for several days. Some people died from poisonous **gas** that rolled down the volcano's sides. Others died from suffocation and still others when roofs collapsed under the weight of ash. Excavation and restoration of the city continues, and today the city is a museum: it shows what a Roman city was like just after the time of Julius Caesar.

Naples—a Disaster Waiting to Happen

It is almost certain that Vesuvius will **erupt** violently again. Today, more people would die as so many more people now live close to the volcano. Naples, with a population of one million people, lies as close to Mount Vesuvius as Pompeii, but on the north side of the mountain. Naples' suburbs are gradually spreading up the volcano's sides. A further three million people live close to the volcano. Imagine what it would be like to live close to 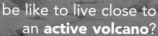 an **active volcano**?

Mount Vesuvius

Vesuvius had erupted many times before the destruction of Pompeii; it is still an active volcano. A major eruption in 1586 killed more people than the one in 79 AD. Vesuvius is a subduction volcano which has built a **composite cone** rising 1281 metres above the nearby Mediterranean Sea and the city of Naples. You can see smoke escaping through the rocks in its crater even when it is not erupting.

What Happens when
Volcanoes Die?

Plume volcanoes die, or become **extinct** as we say, when their plume runs out of heat. **Hotspot volcanoes** die when their crustal plate moves off the **hot spot**. Subduction volcanoes just blow themselves to pieces. Australia has hundreds of dead plume volcanoes and 16 hotspot volcanoes that have become extinct. So Australia is a good place to look at what happens to old volcanoes.

Plugs

As soon as a volcano dies, erosion starts wearing it away. The **ash** and **cinder** goes first, then the softer rocks like **tuff**, then **basalt**, and last of all, the very hard rocks like **trachyte**. When a volcano dies the last **lava** in the **pipe** does not flow to the surface but gets stuck in the pipe and goes solid. This blocking lava is termed a 'plug'. Often this lava is trachyte, the very hard rock. After a very long period of erosion, the trachyte plug may be all that is left of a volcano. The Glasshouse Mountains (Queensland) Mount Warning (New South Wales) and Hanging Rock (Victoria) are all plugs.

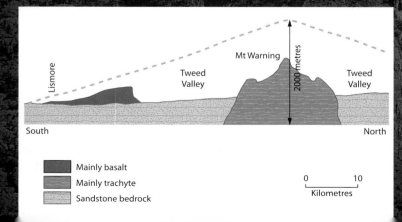

Mainly basalt
Mainly trachyte
Sandstone bedrock

0   10
Kilometres

Only Half Left

The Mount Warning **plug** is as large as all the Glasshouse Mountains put together. The top of Mount Warning is now 1157 metres high, but when it last erupted 20 million years ago its peak was twice as high. Since that last eruption, erosion by the Tweed River has worn away most of the old mountain. The base of the Mount Warning volcano was 100 kilometres wide and some of it extended into the ocean off Tweed Heads.

Chased by a Bear

Old **plugs** are common throughout the world. Devils Tower in the USA rises 386 metres above the surrounding land and has a flat top covered in dry grass and low shrubs. According to an old American Indian legend, some Sioux children were picking flowers in a meadow when they were chased by a giant bear. The Great Spirit felt sorry for the children and lifted up the ground around them to protect them. The bear scratching at the rock trying to reach them made the lines on the side of the tower. I hope the Great Spirit came back to get them down. Do you think he did?

The Breadknife in the Warrumbungles is a wall of trachyte rock over half a kilometre long, 90 metres high and only a few metres wide. It was formed 17 million years ago when lava erupted up through soft rock made of the ash and cinder. The rock cracked open, and the lava filled the crack and solidified. Later the ash and cinder eroded away, leaving the Breadknife standing as we see it today. Why do you think it is called the Breadknife? Can you see the tree growing near its top?

Warrumbungles Plugs

A great variety of volcanic landforms has been revealed in the Warrumbungles (New South Wales) (look for them on the map on page 26) after erosion of the ash, **tuff** and softer rock.

Making Use of
Volcanoes

Throughout the world people are attracted to volcanoes by the rich soil that develops from volcanic **ash** and **lava**. But this is not their only use. People use volcanoes to generate power and for building materials. Volcanoes are also popular tourist destinations.

Insulated pipes from a number of separate well-heads are combined to feed steam through larger pipes to the electricity generators.

Geysers for Generators

Places with lots of geysers make good locations for the generation of electricity. Coal, gas, oil and atomic power stations all generate electricity by heating water in boilers to convert it into steam. The steam is then used to turn the generators, which make electricity. New Zealand, which has many geysers, has a power station at Wairakei on the Volcanic Plateau. It uses steam from within the Earth—the same steam that causes eruptions and geysers—to drive its generators. This power station has been using the renewable non-polluting steam energy from nearby geysers since 1958.

Deep holes are drilled into the hot volcanic rock to reach super-heated water (over 100°C). The hot water and steam is brought to the surface through pipes and collected at the well-heads.

Volcanic Roads

A more common use for old volcanoes is as a source of road-building material. Most asphalt roads have a surface of crushed rock. The most commonly used material for this purpose is the volcanic rock called **basalt**, or as road builders call it, blue metal. Large quarries are located where the rock can be found close to cities. The quarry pictured is at Eagle Hawk, close to Canberra, Australia.

Volcanic Gardens

Scoria is also quarried as a road-building material, but you are more likely to see it in a garden landscape centre. Scoria looks like red gravel and is used in house yards to cover courtyards or place around shrubs and trees. The scoria quarry pictured is at Mount Quincan on the Atherton Tableland in Queensland, Australia.

Volcanic Water Supply

Some **maars** are used as town water supplies. Mount Gambier, a city of more than 20,000 people in South Australia, depends on Blue Lake for its water supply. Blue Lake was formed only 4500 years ago, making it the youngest volcanic feature in Australia. Aborigines lived in the area at that time and stories of the eruptions have been handed down in their oral history. The lake has an average depth of 80 metres. Water flows into the lake through the limestone beneath the city and the lake.

Fertile Farms

Volcanic **ash** breaks down very, very quickly—in as little as 100 years. Soil formed from volcanic ash is very fertile. Farmers in Indonesia, where there are more volcanoes than in any other country, grow their rice in soil made from volcanic ash. The soil is so rich that farmers plant rice right up the sides of many **active volcanoes**. To make the land flat for flooding their rice fields, the farmers have dug terraces with banks around them to hold in the water and grow their crops.

Even single isolated volcanically formed features, such as Milla Milla Falls in Queensland are visited by large numbers of tourists. Can you see the line behind the falls that shows that the small stream is actually flowing over two, not one, lava-flows?

Volcanic Tourism

Each year, millions of tourists flock to volcanic areas for their holidays. Volcanic features such as Yellowstone National Park in the USA, Pompeii in Italy, and Hawaii's Big Island attract more than a million visitors each year. Some of Australia's most popular volcanic sites are national parks like Mount Warning, Undara and the Warrumbungles.

Activities

The Volcano and Earthquake Quiz

1. What makes all the holes in honeycomb lava or rock? (pages 36–37)
2. What is the 'Pacific Ring of Fire'? (pages 22–23)
3. Why do people live on the sides of active volcanoes? (pages 42–43)
4. Why do some buildings fall down in an earthquake and others not? (pages 12–13)
5. What three things make the Earth special and different to the other planets. (pages 6–7)
6. What are the two main metals that make up the core of the Earth? (pages 6–7)
7. From what language does the word 'tsunami' come? (pages 14–15)
8. A seismograph is used for what purpose? (pages 10–11)
9. Name one of the two gases that make volcanoes explode. (pages 20–21)
10. What is the difference between magma and lava? (pages 18–19)
11. Where are the longest lava tubes in the world? (pages 24–25)
12. The presence of small quantities of what metal in lava rock causes soil to turn red? (pages 36–37)
13. Why would you look for diamonds near a volcano? (pages 36–37)
14. Where is the world's largest volcano? (pages 6–7)

Things to Do

1. Draw a picture of a tsunami crashing into a building.
2. Write your story of how you escaped from the giant bear in the legend of Devils Tower's creation. (page 41)
3. Describe your climb to and around the summit of Mount Ngauruhoe and your experiences along the way. What happened on the way down when the volcano began to rumble? (page 23)
4. With some friends develop a drill to save yourself if an earthquake suddenly shook your place. Practise that drill.
5. Make a model of a volcanic cone using plasticine.

44

Glossary (what words mean)

Aa lava	Hawaiian term used to describe solidified lava with a rough clinker-like surface.
Active volcano	One that has erupted in recent times and is likely to erupt again in the future.
Ash	Lightweight honeycombed pulverised volcanic rock ejected from a volcano and having a diameter of less than 2 millimetres.
Atmosphere	The envelope of gas that surrounds a planet or other heavenly body. On earth it is called 'air'.
Basalt	Dark grey volcanic rock generally rich in iron and magnesium. Australia's most common volcanic rock.
Block	Solid rock, with a diameter of greater than 60 millimetres, ejected from a volcanic vent during an eruption.
Bomb	Molten rock, with a diameter of greater than 60 millimetres, ejected from volcanic vent during an eruption.
Caldera	Large volcanic crater formed when a volcanic cone collapses inwards.
Cinder	Lightweight honeycombed pulverised rock ejected from a volcano and having a diameter of 2–60 millimetres.
Cinder cone	A volcanic cone formed of ash and cinder by fountaining.
Composite cone	Steep-sided volcanic cone formed from alternating layers of lava and tephra.
Convection current	A current in a liquid or gas caused by differences in temperature. Hot matter expands, becomes less dense and rises. Cold matter contracts, becomes more dense and sinks.
Core	The partly solid, partly liquid region at the centre of the Earth composed of mainly iron and nickel.
Crater lake	a lake of water in the vent of a dormant or extinct volcano.
Crust	The thin layer of solid rock that forms the surface of the Earth.
Crustal plates	Large sections of the Earth's crust, some larger than continents, that float and move slowly on the underlying mantle.
Dome	Large, steep-sided mass of volcanic rock formed from thick lava that has built up around a volcanic vent.
Dormant	A volcano that has not erupted for a long time, but may still erupt some time in the future.
Dust	Fine volcanic rock with a diameter of less than 0.1 millimetre
Dyke	When magma pushes its way up through cracks in rock, or through tephra, and then solidifies, it is called a dyke.
Erode	The wearing away of rock and soil by running water, glaciers and the wind.
Erupt	The action of lava and/or gas being ejected from a volcanic vent.
Extinct	A volcano that is dead.
Fault	A break in the Earth's crust along which horizontal and/or vertical movement occurs.
Folding	The buckling of part of the Earth's crust.
Fountaining	The rapid release of gas from a volcanic vent that causes particles of lava and lava froth to be hurled into the atmosphere.
Gases (volcanic)	Water vapour, carbon dioxide and other gases contained within magma.
Generator	A machine used to make electricity.
Geologist	A person who studies rocks.
Geology	The study of rocks and their formation.

Geyser	A jet of steam and/or hot water blown into the air by water heated to above 100°C by underlying hot rock.
Greenhouse gases	Gases in the atmosphere such as carbon dioxide, methane and water vapour that hold extra heat in the air, causing the climate to warm.
Hot spot	An area on the Earth's crust located above a rising plume of hot mantle material.
Hotspot volcano	A volcano located above a hot spot.
Lava bomb	See **bomb**.
Lava-flow	A river or flood of molten rock coming from a volcano.
Lava froth	Molten rock bubbles that form on churning lava during the release of volcanic gases.
Lava	Magma after it has reached the surface.
Lava lake	Lake of molten lava lying within a volcanic crater.
Lava reservoir	Body of magma lying below the surface. A larva reservoir may feed one or more volcanoes.
Lava tube	Tunnel formed within a lava-flow when the surface solidifies, permitting lava to continue flowing beneath the crusted surface.
Maar	Volcanic crater formed by an explosion of steam.
Magma	Molten rock which lies below the surface.
Mantle	Layer of the Earth between the core and the crust.
Mantle current	A slow-moving convection current within the Earth's mantle.
Mantle plumes	Streams of heat moving upward through the mantle to the crust.
Molten	A rock or mineral that is heated to a temperature where it changes from a solid to a liquid.
Neck	See **plug**.
Obsidian	Volcanic glass.
Pahoehoe	Hawaiian term used to describe solidified lava that has a smooth or ropy surface.
Pipe	The tube that leads from a lava reservoir through a volcano to the surface.
Plates	See **crustal plates**.
Plug	Solidified lava that fills a volcanic pipe after an eruption ceases.
Plume	See **mantle plume**.
Pumice	Light rock formed from solidified lava froth.
Rift	A break in the Earth's crust caused by two plates moving away from one another.
Ropy lava	Pahoehoe lava with a crinkled surface that looks like coiled rope.
Scoria	Red volcanic cinder coloured by the presence of iron.
Seismograph	Instrument used to measure the force (size) of an earthquake.
Spatter	Volcanic bombs that have partially flattened or distorted on impact with the ground.
Spatter cone	Small volcanic cone built from spatter.
Shield volcano	A low-angled volcanic cone formed mainly from very liquid lava-flows.
Solidified	To change from a molten state to that of a solid.
Subduction	The forcing of a crustal plate down into the mantle.
Tephra	A collective term covering all material blasted from a volcano into the atmosphere. It includes dust, ash, cinder, blocks and bombs.
Trachyte	Common speckled light-coloured volcanic rock that is resistant to weathering and erosion.
Tuff	Rock formed from compressed tephra.
Tsunami	A giant sea wave caused by an earthquake, undersea landslide or volcanic eruption.
Vent	Opening in the Earth's crust through which lava, tephra and gases reach the surface.
Vesicular rock	Honeycombed lava containing a large number of small gas bubbles.
Weathering	The breakdown or decay of rock and rocky material to form soil.

Want to Know More?

Books

Atkinson, A & Atkinson, V. 1995 *Undara Volcano and its Lava Tubes*. Vernon and Anne Atkinson, Brisbane, Australia.

Birch, W.D. 1994 *Volcanoes in Victoria*. Royal Society of Victoria, Melbourne, Australia.

Decker, R & Decker B. 1989 *Volcanoes*. W.H. Freeman & Co. New York.

Duggan, M.B. & Knutson, J. 1993 *The Warrumbungle Volcano*. Australian Geological Survey Organisation, Canberra.

Ferrett, Russell 2005 *Australia's Volcanoes*. Reed New Holland, Sydney, Australia.

Fox, P. 1994 *Mt Kaputar National Park*. The Beaten Track Press, Sydney, Australia.

NSW National Parks & Wildlife Service 1993 *Mount Warning National Park*. NSW National Parks & Wildlife Service, Sydney, Australia.

Orth, K & King, R. 1990 *The Geology of Tower Hill*. Victorian Department of Industry, Melbourne, Australia.

Sutherland, L. 1995 *The Volcanic Earth*. University of NSW Press, Sydney, Australia.

Sutherland, L. 2003 *Earthquakes and Volcanoes*. Readers Digest, Pleasant, New York, USA.

Websites

http://volcano.und.edu
Volcano World. An easy-to-use comprehensive site with links to many other websites specialising in volcanoes and volcanic eruptions.

www.cln.org/themes/volcanoes.html
A Community Learning Network site.

http://earthquake.usgs.gov/research/
US Geological Survey for a selection of current earthquake activity and links to similar sites.

http://cln.org/themes/tsunamis.html
A Community Learning Network site.

www.cln.org/themes/earthquakes.html

www.surfnetkids.com/tsunami.htm
A comprehensive site with many links to other tsunami sites.

www.tsunami.noaa.gov/kids.html
US site for the National Oceanic and Atmospheric Administration with useful links.

Index